MEGA MACHINES

LEARN ABOUT THINGS THAT GO!

CONTENTS

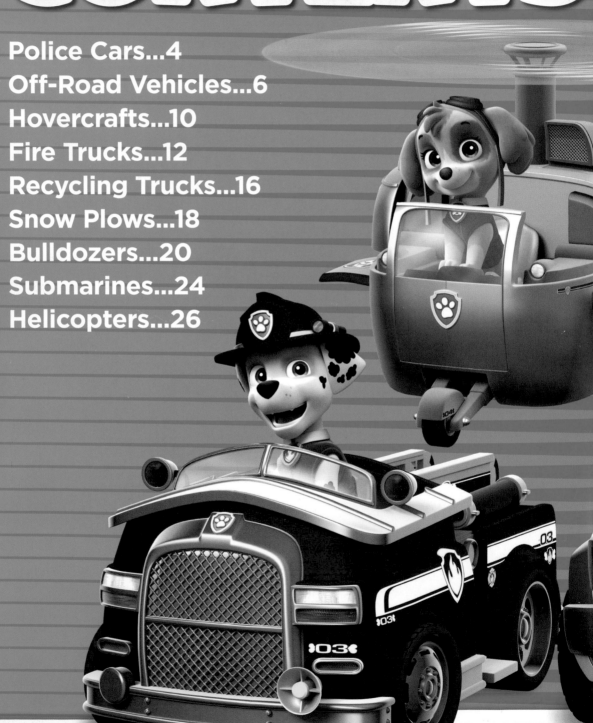

PAW Patrol is on a roll!

The pups of PAW Patrol use their vehicles to help save the day! Discover how their amazing machines put out fires, clear roads, go underwater and more!

Police Cars

Police cars let everyone know the good guys are coming.

Chase is on the case!

Chase's police car has lights, a siren, traffic cones and a winch, which is a special tool for towing other cars!

Police cars have strong bumpers and enhanced engines, steering and electrical systems so they're ready for a high-speed chase!

Off-Road Vehicles

These vehicles can drive almost anywhere.

Follow me!

Tracker's vehicle has really big wheels to help him get around the jungle.

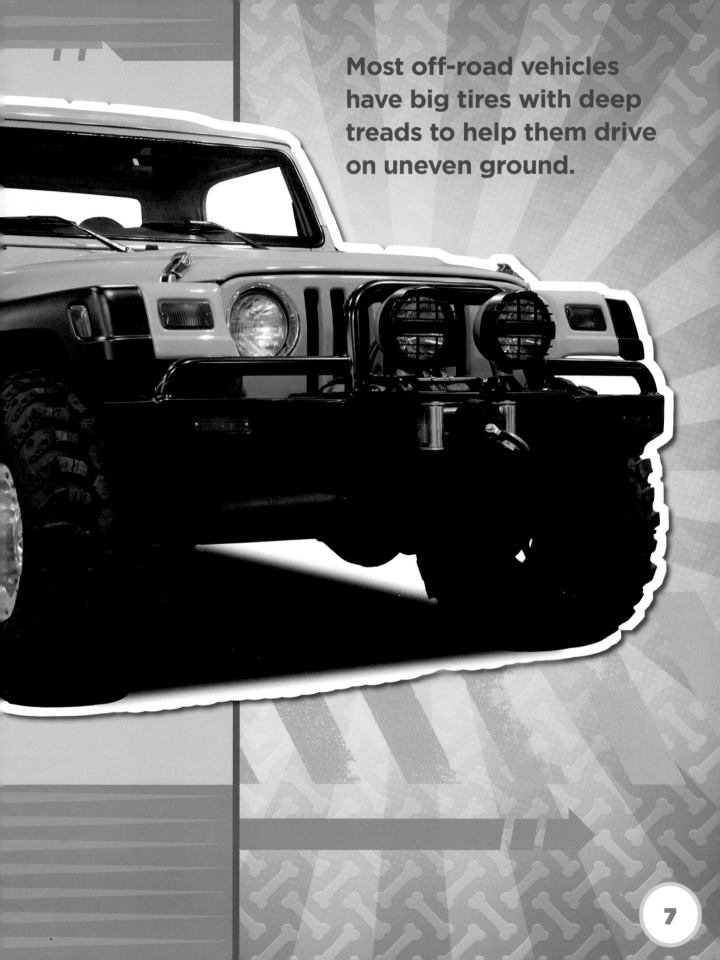

Most off-road vehicles have big tires with deep treads to help them drive on uneven ground.

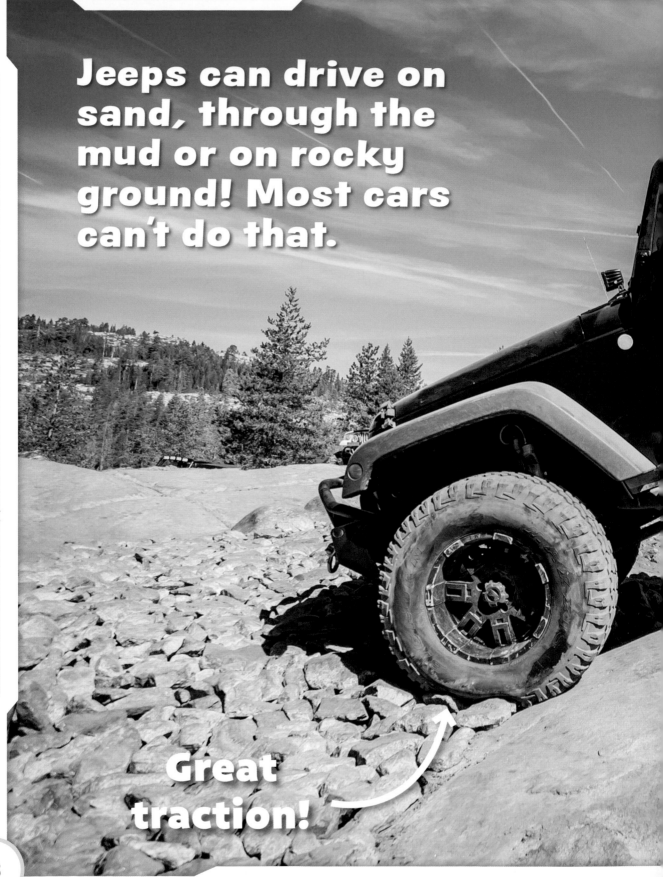

Jeeps can drive on sand, through the mud or on rocky ground! Most cars can't do that.

Great traction!

Not all off-road vehicles are cars. I ride an ATV or all-terrain vehicle! It can climb rocky roads just like a jeep.

Hovercrafts

Hovercrafts can be used
on land and water.

Ready, set, get wet!

Zuma's hovercraft uses
propellers to move forward!

Hovercrafts hover by pushing a lot of air toward the ground!

Fire Trucks

They rush to our aid if someone sees smoke or flames.

I'm fired up!

Marshall's truck has a ladder for reaching high places like roofs, balconies, apartments or even the top of a statue!

Lights and sirens!

These trucks have powerful water hoses for putting out fires!

TRUCK

Ready for a ruff ruff rescue!

Recycling Trucks

Recycling trucks haul items that can be reused instead of throwing them away.

Why trash it when you can stash it?

Rocky's truck has pallet loaders for picking up large items.

Most recycling trucks can collect from up to 500 houses before they're full!

Snowplows

To keep drivers safe, these mighty machines clear snow and ice from roads!

Ice or snow, here we go!

Everest's snowcat has a claw for moving big objects and a medical sled for injured people and animals.

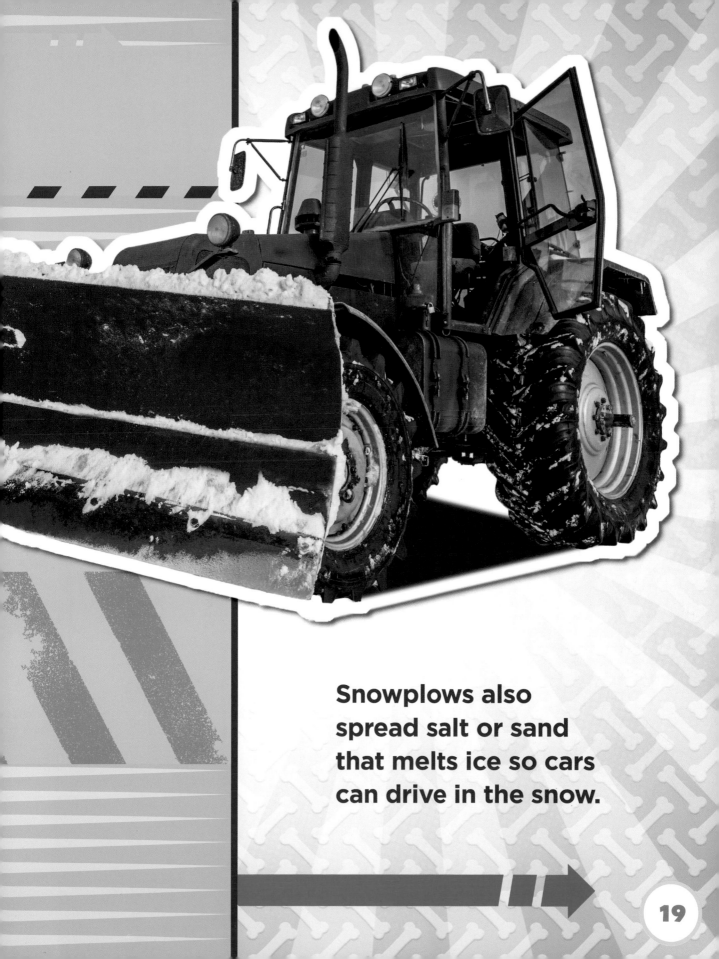

Snowplows also spread salt or sand that melts ice so cars can drive in the snow.

Bulldozers

Bulldozers are really useful on construction sites.

Rubble on the double!

Rubble's bulldozer has lots of neat tools, including a digger scoop, a claw arm and a crane.

Bulldozers have big wheels or tracks to give them good balance and traction.

Submarines

Submarines are used for exploring underwater.

Let's dive in!

Zuma's boat can turn into a submarine! It has a claw attachment to help him grab things he finds in the bay!

24

Submarines travel underwater for scientific research, to look for items lost in shipwrecks and even for military operations!

Helicopters

Helicopters are flying vehicles that are used for transportation and rescue missions when an airplane is too big.

Let's take to the sky!

Skye's helicopter has a harness and cable to pick up and carry objects.

Helicopters have special propellers so they can fly in one spot and make tight turns.

DANGER KEEP AWAY

Ready for take-off!

28

A chopper's cable in action!

Machines are awesome!

Remember, no vehicle is too big, no pup is too small!

Media Lab Books
For inquiries, call 646-838-6637

Copyright 2017 Topix Media Lab

Published by Topix Media Lab
14 Wall Street, Suite 4B
New York, NY 10005

Printed in China

ISBN-10: 1-942556-69-1
ISBN-13: 978-1-942556-69-5

CEO Tony Romando

Vice President of Brand Marketing Joy Bomba
Director of Finance Vandana Patel
Director of Sales and New Markets Tom Mifsud
Manufacturing Director Nancy Puskuldjian
Financial Analyst Matthew Quinn
Brand Marketing Assistant Taylor Hamilton

Editor-in-Chief Jeff Ashworth
Creative Director Steven Charny
Photo Director Dave Weiss
Managing Editor Courtney Kerrigan
Senior Editors Tim Baker, James Ellis

Content Editor Kaytie Norman
Content Designer Rebecca Stone
Content Photo Editor Catherine Armanasco
Art Director Susan Dazzo
Assistant Managing Editor Holland Baker
Senior Designer Michelle Lock
Designer Danielle Santucci
Assistant Photo Editor Jessica Ariel Wendroff
Assistant Editors Trevor Courneen, Alicia Kort
Editorial Assistant Isabella Torchia

Co-Founders Bob Lee, Tony Romando

p5 Mark Reinstein/Getty Images; p7 Oleksiy Maksymenko/Alamy; p17 Scott Olson/Getty images; p19 Violeta Chalakova/iStock;
p22 kadmy/iStock; p28 Dan Barnes/iStock; Shutterstock: cover, p8, 11, 13, 14, 21, 25, 27, back cover.

PAW Patrol is on a roll!